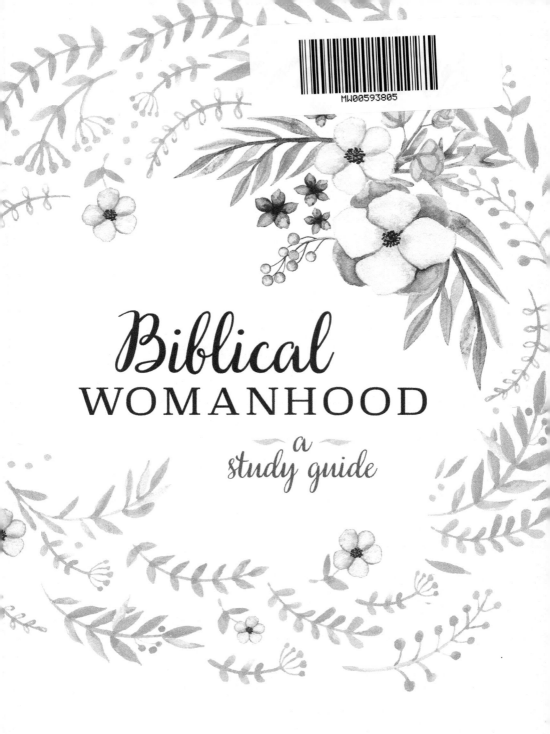

Biblical
WOMANHOOD

a
study guide

LORI ALEXANDER
author of *The Power of a Transformed Wife*

Cover and interior design by Blue Muse Studio (www.bluemusestudio.com)

For information on Lori Alexander, visit her blog at www.thetransformedwife.com.

To contact her, please email her at thetransformedwife7@gmail.com.

Table of Contents

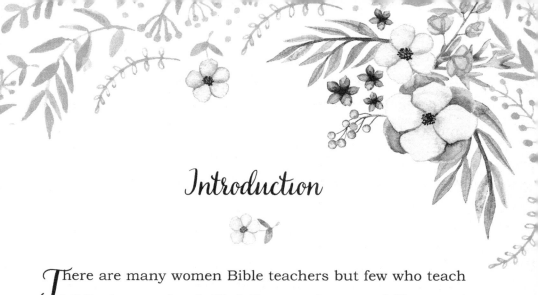

Introduction

*T*here are many women Bible teachers but few who teach biblical womanhood. Christian marriages are falling apart at an alarming rate. Children are being raised by strangers instead of by loving and nurturing mothers. They are being sent away to government-run schools all of their childhood where teachers aren't allowed to teach anything about the Lord and His ways. Most women don't know that they are the ones who God has commanded to be keepers at home and raise their own children. Teenagers raised in Christian homes are walking away from their faith in high numbers. Thus, the reason I write this study.

I would love to see churches all over begin to have the older women teaching the younger women the ways of biblical womanhood as commanded in Titus 2:3-5. There would be classes where a few older women would gather around a circle with younger women and begin to teach them the ways of the Lord. They would teach them how to have strong marriages, raise godly children, be keepers at home, learn the ways of homemaking, dress modestly, and teach them to be women after God's own heart. The young women can ask the older women questions and learn from their experiences and wisdom.

This is a twelve-week course intended to teach young women what God wants them to be taught about biblical womanhood. The Church needs older women to step up to the plate and begin obeying God in this area. What if older women feel disqualified? If you are a godly, older woman, you ARE qualified according to God! Here are the qualifications for older women: "that they be in behavior, not false accusers, not given to much wine, teachers of good things" (Titus 2:3) and the "good things" they are commanded to teach are listed in Titus 2:4, 5.

"That they may teach the young women to be sober, to love their husband, to love their children, to be discreet, chaste, keepers at home, good, obedient to their own husbands, that the word of God be not blasphemed."

I will also be using verses from Proverbs 31 and other verses in the Bible that specifically have to do with biblical womanhood. I pray this will be encouraging and enriching to the older women as well as the young women. I know that as I have taught young women, it has caused me to examine myself and my own actions more closely. It has also convicted and challenged me. God's Word has a way of doing this!

"For the word of God is quick, and powerful, and sharper than any twoedged sword, piercing even to the dividing asunder of soul and spirit, and of the joints and marrow, and is a discerner of the thoughts and intents of the heart" (Hebrews 4:12).

I will be mostly using the King James Version of the Bible and the 1828 Webster Dictionary. You can get both of these as apps on your smartphones.

Study #1

BE SOBER

*Y*oung women are to be sober. Sober means "habitually temperate, not intoxicated or overpowered; not drunken; not heated with passion, having a sound mind." We are also commanded to be temperate in all things (1 Corinthians 9:25). Temperate means "moderate in the indulgences of the appetites and passions; as temperate in eating and drinking; temperate in pleasures; temperate in speech; disciplined."

Why did God put being sober as the first in the list of qualities that He wants young women to pursue? Without discipline and a sound mind, it would be impossible to obey the following commands and walk after the Spirit. We are not to be drunk with wine but to be filled with the Spirit (Ephesians 5:18). With His Spirit working mightily within us and continually renewing our minds with God's Truth found in His Word, we will be transformed into His image (Romans 12:1, 2)!

I decided a few years ago that I wasn't going to drink any more alcohol. I am a lightweight when it comes to alcohol. I don't feel well when I consume even a little bit and I don't want to be a stumbling block to others (1 Corinthians 8:9). It's not a sin to drink alcohol but just remember, if you are going to drink alcohol, be sure you remain sober at all times and never get drunk; for this is forbidden in Scripture.

Would you consider yourself to be a sober person?

Do you aim to be moderate in your appetite and how much alcohol do you drink if you do drink? ....

....

Are you temperate in your pleasures: cell phone usage, television watching, eating, shopping, etc.? ....

....

....

Does your cell phone or the television control you or do you control them? ....

....

....

We are not to be mastered by anything (no, not even our emotions) but by Christ. Write out 1 Corinthians 6:12. ....

....

....

....

Using the cell phone, drinking wine, watching TV and going to movies, dancing, and many other things are lawful for us but are they profitable? You must ponder this question concerning many areas of your life and make sure that you don't allow anything to have control over you except for the Holy Spirit.

"But I keep under my body, and bring it into subjection: lest that by any means, when I have preached to others, I myself should be a castaway" (1 Corinthians 9:27).

Look up these verses about being sober and write a brief description for each one. The Word of God is what transforms us so you will be in the Word a lot during this study! Don't skip this part.

Romans 12:3

2 Corinthians 5:13

1 Thessalonians 5:6

1 Thessalonians 5:8

1 Timothy 3:2

Titus 2:12

1 Peter 1:13

1 Peter 4:7 ....

....

....

1 Peter 5:8 ....

....

....

Looking back on what masters you, what are some steps that
you can take to master them instead? ....

....

....

....

Who specifically is commanded to be sober in the following
verses?

1 Timothy 3:2 ....

....

....

1 Timothy 3:11 ....

....

....

Titus 1:7, 8 ....

....

....

Titus 2:2 ....

....

....

Titus 2:4

Titus 2:6

God makes it very obvious that He commands all age groups and positions in the churches to be sober and sober-minded. There is no guess work here. If this is important to Him, it must be important to us because all of His ways are good, and acceptable, and perfect!

Study #2

LOVE YOUR HUSBAND

$\mathcal{T}$rue biblical love is not a feeling or an emotion, women. Just as your love for God was a choice, your love for your husband needs to be a daily choice. Here's how God's Word defines love in 1 Corinthians 13 using the NASB:

"Love is patient, love is kind and is not jealous; love does not brag and is not arrogant, does not act unbecomingly; it does not seek its own, is not provoked, does not take into account a wrong suffered, does not rejoice in unrighteousness, but rejoices with the truth; bears all things, believes all things, hopes all things, endures all things. Love never fails."

Many women today are heavily involved in their churches. They go to the women's Bible study. They serve when there is a need. They go to church every Sunday and lift their hands up in praise. They help at the closest homeless shelter and are generous with their money, yet they come home and are unkind and ill-tempered towards their husbands. The above verses tell us that all of those "good" things these women are doing amount to nothing if they are not loving their husbands.

Did you notice that there is NOTHING in these verses about emotions and feelings? It is also not dependent upon how your husband treats you. You are only responsible for your own behavior, not that of your husband's. Are you patient towards him? ....

....

Are you kind towards him?

....

Read 1 Corinthians 3:1-3. What are some words that describe those who cause strife and divisions?

....

....

....

....

I don't know about you but I would rather not be known as a "babe in Christ" or "carnal," would you? There are several verses in Proverbs about quarreling and contentious wives. Let's determine to no longer quarrel or argue with our husbands and walk after the Spirit instead. (You may have to bite your tongue often!)

Go through the description of love in 1 Corinthians 13 and ask yourself if you are loving your husband as God commands that you love him. I have often heard that God commands husbands to love their wives as Christ loves the Church but there are no commands for wives to love their husbands. Even a popular book on marriage claimed this to be true but it's false! Wives are commanded to love their husbands.

All throughout the Word of God we are commanded to love others and this includes our husbands. We are told in 1 John 4:8 that if we don't love, we do not know God. If we don't love our husbands, then we need to examine our faith (2 Corinthians 13:5).

What are the qualities that caused you to "fall in love" with your husband?

....

....

....

....

Do you still admire those qualities and do you choose to focus upon them rather than upon his faults?

....

....

....

....

....

What do you do if you have critical thoughts about him?

....

....

....

....

....

We are told to bring "into captivity every thought to the obedience of Christ" (2 Corinthians 10:5). Every time you have a negative thought that comes into your mind, simply take it to Christ and kick the negative thought out!

Read 1 Peter 3:8-11 and give some ways that are given in these verses on how to show love to others.

....

....

....

....

Love has much more to do with actions than with words. "Let us not love in word, neither in tongue; but in deed and in truth" (1 John 3:18). What are some ways that you love your husband with actions? ....

....

....

....

....

....

What should a married woman care for according to 1 Corinthians 7:34? ....

....

....

....

....

What are some ways that you can please your husband?

....

....

....

....

Ask this of yourself and be honest: Do you love your husband as God has called you to love him? If you answer no, how can you begin to obey God in this area? ....

....

....

....

Finally, continually remind yourselves that God's Spirit works in you mightily and you can do all things through Christ who strengthens you!

Study #3
LOVE YOUR CHILDREN

Our culture doesn't love children. There are over a million abortions every year. Children are being raised by strangers most of their lives. Many mothers aren't the ones home with their children full time nurturing, disciplining, and caring for their children. Mothers need to learn and be taught how to love their children.

Look up Deuteronomy 6:6, 7. How often and where are we to teach our children the ways of the Lord?

In Proverbs 22:6, we are told to train up a child in the way they should go and when they are old, they will not depart from it. Are you consistently training your children in the way they should go?

Are you dealing with the foolishness in them immediately?

Look up Proverbs 22:15 and see how God wants parents to deal with foolishness in a child. It's a lot harder when they are older so deal with it when they are young.

Spanking is a controversial issue these days yet it never was up until this present generation. All fifty states in the United States still allow parents to spank their children with something other than their hand at the time of this writing but make sure to check with your state or country to see if it is legal. This doesn't include abuse in any form: pulling of the hair, slapping a child on the face, whipping a child on the back, or punching in the stomach. The best and safest place to spank a young child is on the bottom or upper thigh. Read the following verses and summarize what God has to say about the rod.

Proverbs 13:24 ....

....

....

Proverbs 23:13 ....

....

....

Proverbs 29:15 ....

....

....

How does God discipline us according to Hebrews 12:6? ....

....

....

What does "chasten" mean according to the dictionary?

What does "scourge" mean?

God commands children to do what in Ephesians 6:1 and Colossians 3:20?

Whose responsibility is it to teach your children to obey you?

I cannot overemphasize how important it is to train and discipline your children to obey you. There's a much greater chance that your children will grow up to obey the Lord if you do, but make sure you are consistently giving them a lot of affection and praise, too.

The verses in Ephesians 6:4 and Colossians 3:21 warn husbands not to do something to their children. What is it?

....

....

....

....

Provoke means to make angry. How might you or your husband provoke your children to anger?

....

....

....

....

One of the greatest ways to not provoke your children to wrath is to love their daddy and stay married to him until death do you part. Divorce causes children to grow up angry and bitter.

The first few years of a child's life (from one to about three years) are crucial to training and disciplining your child. Teach them the meaning of "no" early. Teach them to obey you immediately when asked something by you or told to stop something. Be consistent and firm. After spanking them for openly disobeying you, cuddle with them, tell them you love them, and why you had to discipline them. It's more about disciplining them to do right than punishing them for doing wrong, but they do work together.

You want children who grow up to walk in truth. "I have no greater joy than to hear that my children walk in truth" (3

John 4). I have seen too many women being permissive with their children when they were young and these children grow up to be rebellious when they are older. Give them the gift of self-discipline and self-control by disciplining the rebellion out of them when they are young.

God commands young women to "marry, bear children, and guide the home" (1 Timothy 5:14). This is His will for most young women. Many women today put off marrying for higher education and careers instead of getting married and having children. Children are an important part of God's will for women.

"Lo, children are an heritage of the Lord: and the fruit of the womb is his reward. As arrows are in the hand of a mighty man; so are children of the youth. Happy is the man that hath his quiver full of them: they shall not be ashamed, but they shall speak with the enemies in the gate" (Psalm 127:3-5).

What is a similar occupation that older widows are to be known for and young women are commanded to do in 1 Timothy 5:10 and 5:14?

....

....

Read Psalm 127:3-5. What are children according to verse 3?

....

....

Children are a heritage of the LORD and a reward! Yes, God values children greatly.

What are children compared to in verse 4?

What two adjectives are used to describe a man who has a quiver full of children?

How are a wife and children described in Psalm 128:3?

Do you want to be a fruitful vine by the sides of your home?

Are you open to having children and raising them in the nurture and the admonition of the Lord?

If fear is the reason you don't want children, learn to live a life of faith instead of fear. Trust in your Creator that if He blesses you with children, He will provide for them and give you the strength needed to raise them.

Today, many young women leave their babies in the care of others so they can have their careers. Your babies need you! When they are clingy to you around nine to 18 months and want no one else, this is normal. This is when they are bonding to their mothers and will help them to grow up to be emotionally stable and secure. (Read "The Way Home" by Mary Pride to learn more about the importance of being home full time with your children.)

Who can raise your children better than you? Why has God given these children specifically to you?

....

....

....

Most Christian parents send their children away to government-run schools all of their childhoods. These schools aren't allowed to teach your children about the Lord or His ways. There is no wisdom taught in the public schools. In fact, they teach things that are opposed to the ways of the Lord. Do you believe this is what the Lord wants for your children?

....

....

Read 2 Corinthians 6:14-18. Briefly explain God's opinion about mixing His children with those of the world. How does it match up with how you are raising your children?

....

....

....

How do you think Christian parents were convinced that sending their children away from the safety and security of their homes to be raised by strangers, who aren't allowed to mention the name of God, was a good thing?

....

....

....

Why do you think God wants you to be the one raising your children, that He blessed you with, full time?

....

....

....

What are the benefits to homeschooling your children?

....

....

....

Remember, "bad company corrupts good morals" (1 Corinthians 15:33). Do you want your children's peers to have a greater influence upon your children or are you the one God calls to influence your children towards godliness?

....

....

....

Remember, their eternal souls are all that matters in the end.

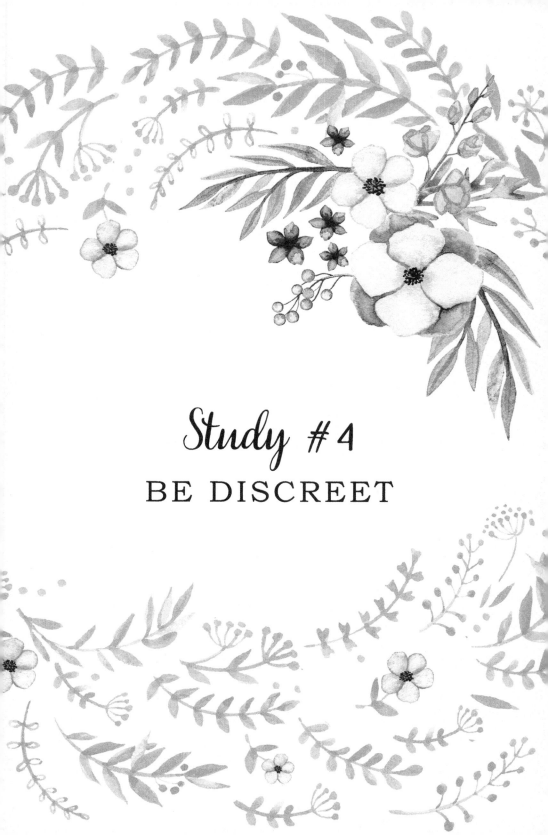

Study #4

BE DISCREET

Discreet means "prudent; wise in avoiding errors or evil, and in selecting the best means to accomplish a purpose; circumspect; cautious, wary; not rash."

In Genesis 41:33 and in Genesis 41:39, what word is matched up with the word discreet?

Would you consider yourself a wise woman and where does wisdom come from? Look up Proverbs 2:6, 7 for your answer.

How do we get wisdom? Look up James 1:5.

The only way you will become a wise woman is by being in the Word of God consistently since all wisdom comes from God. We are told that we are transformed by renewing our minds with truth (Romans 12:1). Have you disciplined yourself to be in the Word almost every day?

If so, what does this time with the Lord look like? Share this with the others if you would like!

In order to be discreet, you must be wise. You must daily ask the Lord for wisdom.

Look up Proverbs 11:22. What does the LORD compare a woman to that has no discretion? ....

....

Look up Proverbs 7:11. How is a harlot described in this verse?

....

....

Give the opposite words of those that describe a harlot?

"loud" ....

"stubborn" ....

"feet not abide in her house" ....

....

Harlots are the opposite of being discreet. May we never have any quality traits that harlots have.

"Ponder the paths of thy feet, and let all thy ways be established" (Proverbs 4:26). Do you ponder your paths? ....

....

How do young women today lack discretion and how can you, as godly a woman, do better? ....

....

....

....

....

What about ways you act in front of your husband? Are you feminine and discreet in front of him? Do you do your best to not do those things that your husband may not find attractive?

....

....

....

Do you use discretion in the words that you say and the way you talk with people? ....

....

Look up Ephesians 4:29. How does the Lord instruct us to speak to others? ....

....

....

Women are to be discreet in the way they dress. Look up 1 Timothy 2:9, 10. What are women to adorn themselves with?

....

....

We are told to adorn ourselves with modest apparel. This doesn't only mean to make sure we are covered up and not causing men to stumble, but as reaffirmed later in the verse by the phrase "not with...costly array." Look up the word "modest." What is the definition? ....

....

....

....

....

Our culture feeds the lust in women to stay in fashion since fashions are always changing. It also feeds the lust for women to be sexy. Neither of these are from the LORD. He wants us to be known for moderation even in the amount of clothing we buy and the amount of money we spend on them. God also wants us to be "shamefaced" which means not trying to draw attention to ourselves. We want to draw others to Christ in us, not ourselves.

Look up 1 Corinthians 9:25. What defines a man or woman who strives for mastery?

....

....

Temperate means "moderate in the indulgence of the appetites and passions and showing self-restraint." We should not strive to dress and act like the culture around us. We are commanded to "not be conformed to this world" (Romans 12:2). Our clothing should be modest and fashions ought not consume us. We don't want to dress in a way that attracts undue attention towards us, either. What does God want us to adorn ourselves with in 1 Timothy 2:10?

....

....

....

What are some good works that you do?

....

....

....

Your good works please God. They make you more beautiful to God than anything you can wear!

Look up 1 Peter 3:4, 5. In these verses, we are also told what we, as godly women, should adorn ourselves with? What are they?

....

....

....

Are you discreet in the way you dress? Do you draw attention to yourself in the way you dress or act?

....

....

....

....

The best way to know if you are modest or not is to ask your husband. He is a man and he clearly knows what can cause a man to lust and what is modest. We don't want to act or dress in a way that may cause men to stumble but to dress in a way that brings glory to God.

Study #5

BE CHASTE

Chaste means to be "pure from all unlawful commerce of sexes. Applied to persons before marriage, it signifies pure from all sexual commerce, undefiled; applied to married persons, true to the marriage bed; free from obscenity; in language, pure genuine; uncorrupt."

There are only three verses in the Bible that mentions the word "chaste." Look them up and summarize them.

2 Corinthians 11:2 ....

....

....

Titus 2:5 ....

....

....

1 Peter 3:2 ....

....

....

"Conversation" in 1 Peter 3:2 refers to one's behavior and general course of manners.

What can keep us from being "chaste virgins to Christ" according to 2 Corinthians 11:2, 3? ....

....

....

....

In order for our minds to not be corrupted, we must study and know the truth of God's Word so when we hear false teachings, we will immediately know that it's false. We must also "take every thought captive to the obedience of Christ" (2 Corinthians 10:5).

What are we to dwell on according to Philippians 4:8? ....

....

....

What warnings are we told about women in 2 Timothy 3:6, 7 who aren't strong in their faith and don't know the Word of God? ....

....

....

Not only are we to be chaste in our minds and be careful who we learn from and what we dwell upon, we must be chaste in our words and actions. Look up 1 Timothy 5:13. What are some things that young women have a tendency to do?

....

....

Seeing the characteristics that God doesn't want defining young women, what are the opposite of these:

"Learn to be idle" ....

....

"Wandering from house to house" ....

....

"Tattlers" ....

....

God's will for young women is to work hard at home and not
gossip about other people. What does He want them to talk
about? Look up Ephesians 4:29 and summarize. ....

....

....

....

What does Colossians 4:6 say about our speech? ....

....

....

We are also called to be chaste when it comes to sexual inti-
macy. What does Hebrews 13:4 say about the marriage bed?

....

....

....

Your husband is the only one you are to have sexual relations
with. Read 1 Corinthians 7:1-5. God gives clear instructions
in these verses for the sexual relationship between a husband and a wife. How are we to avoid fornication according
to verse 2? ....

....

....

What are we to clearly give to our husbands according to
verse 3? ....

....

"Benevolence" is the desire to promote their happiness and disposition to do good. Your desire should be to do good towards your husband and promote his happiness. Most men thoroughly enjoy sex and it makes them happy!

Who has power over your body according to verse 4?

....

....

What is God's command to us concerning sexual relations with our husband in verse 5?

....

....

"Defraud" means to "deprive of right and to withhold wrongfully from another what is due to him." We are NOT to withhold sex from our husband. He has power over our body, according to God, so give sex willingly and freely to your husband. Make him very happy!

What can happen IF we defraud our husband according to verse 5?

....

....

....

Do everything in your power to keep your husband from being tempted by Satan. Now, this is no guarantee that he won't look at pornography nor have an affair but, at least, you will know that you are doing what God has called you to do.

Study #6

KEEPERS AT HOME

This topic is the one that I receive the most criticism for teaching. Most churches don't teach young women to be keepers at home. It's not popular in our day and age to teach women to be home with their children instead of having a career, but it's what God commands older women to teach young women so I do.

Where is a woman commanded to work in the Bible? Look up these verses:

Titus 2:5

1 Timothy 5:14

Psalm 113:9

The Proverbs 31 woman wasn't known for having a career or making money. She did not leave her home for hours every day and her children in the care of others to work for a boss. Many want to believe she was a career woman but this is a modern-day fable.

What are the two things she was known for in Proverbs 31:27?

1. ....

2. ....

What was she praised for in verses 30 and 31? ....

....

....

....

....

How important is working hard for the Lord? Look up the following verses and summarize:

Colossians 3:23 ....

....

....

Proverbs 13:4 ....

....

....

What were some of the specific activities the Proverbs 31 woman did in and around her home and how can we relate them to things women can do in and around their homes?

Proverbs 31:13 ....

....

....

Proverbs 31:14 ....

....

....

Proverbs 31:15 ....

....

Proverbs 31:20 ....

....

Proverbs 31:22 ....

....

Proverbs 31:24 ....

....

It wasn't her coworkers and boss who rose up and called her
blessed. Who was it in Proverbs 31:28? ....

....

....

What is the different between a foolish woman and a wise
woman in Proverbs 14:1? ....

....

....

List some ways that a foolish woman can tear down her home?

....

....

....

Now, list some ways that a wise woman can build her home up?

....

....

....

....

Are you a wise woman who is building her home up or a foolish one who is tearing her home down with her own hands?

....

....

....

If you are a single mother who has no choice but to work outside of your home, take it daily to the Lord in prayer; for He cares for you. Lay your requests at His feet and trust that He is working it out. Ask Him for wisdom and search out possible ways for you to make money from home; for nothing is impossible with Him! In the meantime, know that His strength and grace are sufficient.

Study #7

BE GOOD

In Titus 2:4-5, older women are commanded to teach young women to be good. People will exclaim, "But none of us are good, no, not one!" No, we aren't "good" until we are filled with His Spirit and made new creatures in Christ but everyone, whether saved or not, has the choice to do good or not. Most parents teach their children to do and be good, likewise, older women are to teach young women to be good.

The most important part of being good as believers in Jesus Christ is walking in the Spirit. Look up these verses about how we are to walk and you will get a good idea about what walking in the Spirit looks like.

Romans 4:12

Romans 6:4

Romans 13:13

2 Corinthians 5:7

Galatians 5:16

Ephesians 2:10

Ephesians 4:1

Ephesians 4:17

Ephesians 5:2

Ephesians 5:8

Ephesians 5:15

Colossians 1:10

Colossians 2:6

Colossians 4:5

1 Thessalonians 2:12

1 Thessalonians 4:12

1 John 1:7

2 John 6

3 John 4 ....

....

There are many verses in the Bible with the word "good" in them so I only chose a few. Write out the phrases with the word "good" in them:

Proverbs 2:20 ....

....

Proverbs 11:23 ....

....

Proverbs 11:27 ....

....

Proverbs 12:2 ....

....

Proverbs 14:14 ....

....

Proverbs 17:22 ....

....

As believers in Jesus Christ, it's crucial to know who you are in Christ. Look up these verses and find out who you are in Christ. You are NO longer considered a sinner since this no longer defines you. (Yes, you will sin, but it should no longer be a way of life.) You are considered a saint! This will be the most important part of this entire study!

2 Corinthians 5:17 ....

....

Philippians 4:13

Romans 6:2

Romans 6:4

Romans 6:6

Romans 6:7

Romans 6:8

Romans 6:9

Romans 6:11

Romans 6:14

Romans 6:18

Romans 6:22

Count how many times that we are told that we are either dead to sin or freed from sin?

Romans 7:4 ....

....

Romans 7:6 ....

....

Romans 8:1 ....

....

Romans 8:2 ....

....

Since we have been risen with Christ and are dead and freed from sin and filled with His Holy Spirit who works mightily within us (Colossians 1:29), what are we promised in Philippians 4:13? ....

....

....

....

....

....

I could give many more verses from different books of the Bible in the New Testament to try to convince you about who you are in Christ, but I think you should have a good idea from the verses you looked up. Keep your eyes open to them as you read through the New Testament books, especially from Romans to Revelation since these books were written for the Church age under which we presently live. We are no longer in bondage to our sin. We have His Spirit working in us. Begin believing what God says about you, NOT how you feel about yourself!

It's a whole lot easier to be good when you clearly understand who you are in Christ and believe God in faith. We were never meant to try to be good on our own. This is why He left His Holy Spirit to indwell His children and His written Word to transform us. Now we are new creatures in Christ and are told that we can do all things through Christ who strengthens us!

Study #8

OBEDIENT TO YOUR OWN HUSBAND

omen aren't crazy about this topic but it's God's perfect will for you, women! What is God's ordained order in a marriage? Look up the following verses and write the answers beside it.

Genesis 3:16

1 Corinthians 11:3

1 Corinthians 11:7

1 Corinthians 11:8

1 Corinthians 11:9

Ephesians 5:22

Ephesians 5:23

Ephesians 5:24

Ephesians 5:33

Colossians 3:18 ....

....

1 Peter 3:1 ....

....

1 Peter 3:5 ....

....

1 Peter 3:6 ....

....

In these thirteen verses, God's will and order in marriage is firmly established. There isn't one verse that commands husbands to submit to their wives. There is no such thing as mutual submission in a marriage. Every institution in the world has a leader and God chose the husband to be the leader in the family.

Now, let's take a look at wives who are married to disobedient husbands in 1 Peter 3:1, 2. How are they to try and win their husbands? ....

....

....

....

"Conversation" in the KJV refers to behavior. A disobedient husband should clearly be able to see Christ in his wife, living in and through her by her godly behavior. Therefore, she will want to do all she can to win her husband to the Lord. (We will go into much more detail in the next study.)

What does the Lord command of a godly wife in 1 Corinthians 7:10? ....

....

....

In the next verse, we are given a "but" and "if." Why? ....

....

....

There are times when a wife should not obey her husband. If he asks her to do something evil, such as watch porn with him, rob a bank, or participate in a threesome, she should disobey him. In most everything else, she should obey him since this is God's will for her. How are wives commanded to win husbands who are disobedient to the word? By disobeying them and living as they please? No, but by living in subjection to them, thus obeying them as "Sarah obeyed Abraham" (1 Peter 3:6) as we will study in the next chapter.

Practice obeying him in the little things, too. When he asks for something or wants you to do something for him, do it as soon as you can, not when you feel like doing it. As you obey your husband, you obey the Lord since obeying your husband is what God asks of you. Your husband is your authority and this is good. All of God's ways are good!

Study #9

WINNING A DISOBEDIENT HUSBAND

*Y*our husband may not be a Christian. He may not go to church. He may drink too much alcohol or watch garbage on TV, possibly even pornography. What are women to do in these and others situations like this? (***If you are in an extremely difficult or destructive marriage, please seek help!)

Look up 1 Peter 3:1, 2. How are wives supposed to act towards their husbands in hopes of winning them? ....

....

This is so contrary to how most women would act towards a disobedient husband. They would most likely want to do everything in their own power to change their husbands. The following verses in Proverbs are how NOT to win a husband. Write them out.

Proverbs 19:13 ....

....

Proverbs 21:19 ....

....

Proverbs 27:15 ....

....

Contentious means "given to angry debates; quarrelsome; perverse; stubborn; petulant." These are not ways to win a husband even if he isn't disobedient to the Word! These qualities will push any man away from a wife.

Marriage courses will teach couples how to "fight" fair. Look up these verses and tell me what God thinks about strife.

Proverbs 15:18

....

Proverbs 17:14

....

Proverbs 26:21

....

Proverbs 29:22

....

1 Corinthians 3:3

....

1 Timothy 6:4

....

James 3:16

....

What does God think about us causing strife in our marriage?

....

....

....

We should not fight, quarrel, or have strife in our homes. We don't preach the Word to our husbands. We are not their spiritual leader. We live in submission to them with chaste conversation.

What about that last phrase "coupled with fear" in 1 Peter 3:2? What does this mean? ....

....

....

Look up Ephesians 5:33. What does the second part of this verse teach? ....

....

....

....

Reverence means "fear mingled with respect and esteem." A godly woman fears God and knows His ways are superior to her ways even when they don't make sense and don't appear to be working. She keeps her eyes on the eternal rewards by living in obedience to the Lord with His Spirit working mightily within her. Her greatest desire is to glorify God in everything and store her treasures in heaven, therefore, she continues to reverence her disobedient husband and prays for his salvation.

What are wives commanded not to do in 1 Corinthians 7:10?

....

But and if she departs, then what is she to do according to the next verse? ....

....

....

Yes, there may be times when a wife needs to separate from her husband. If she is being physically abused in any way or perhaps, he is emotionally abusing her through extreme measures of control. In any of these cases, she needs to reach out for help and seek wise counsel.

What about a wife who is married to an unbeliever who is not abusive according to 1 Corinthians 7:13?

....

....

....

....

What is a promise in 1 Corinthians 7:14 that a believing wife can cling to in this type of marriage?

....

....

....

....

This means that as a believing wife is living with her unbelieving husband and children, Jesus is living in the home because He lives in her. There's a much greater chance that her husband and children will become believers as she lives a godly life in front of them.

What happens if the unbelieving husband departs according to 1 Corinthians 7:15?

....

....

....

....

If her husband departs, she must let him go. She can do whatever she can to win him back biblically (1 Peter 3:1-6), but if he divorces her and remarries another, can she remarry according to 1 Corinthians 7:28? ....

....

Is there any promise that a believing wife will win her unbelieving husband in 1 Corinthians 7:16? ....

....

If an unbelieving husband doesn't leave his believing wife, what is God's will for her and all married believers according to 1 Corinthians 7:39? ....

....

....

The only sure way a believing wife can remarry is if her husband divorces her and remarries or if her husband dies. (Some believe a wife can remarry if her husband divorces her and abandons her while wanting nothing to do with her. I believe this is true but others will disagree.)

Yes, fornication is given for a reason to divorce in Matthew 5:32 but divorce should be the last option for believers in Jesus Christ. Many marriages have been restored after an affair. Remember that the reason Moses gave for divorce was due to the hardness of the heart (Matthew 19:8) which no believer should have since we are to forgive others as Christ has forgiven us. I will never encourage a woman to divorce her husband since his eternal soul is what may be at stake.

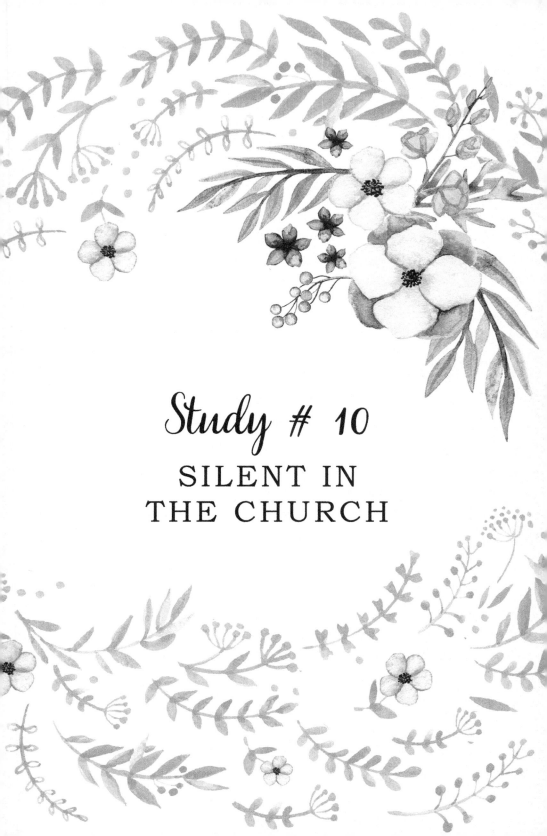

Study # 10

SILENT IN
THE CHURCH

$\mathcal{M}$any will try to convince you that the following commands to women are no longer applicable because the Apostle Paul was only writing to a particular church but this is not so. Women are no better behaved today than when he wrote his epistles!

Look up 1 Corinthians 14:33 and explain who Paul was specifically writing to at this time?

In the next two verses (1 Corinthians 14:34, 35), what five clear instructions does he give about women's behavior in the churches?

1.

2.

3.

4.

5.

Now, turn to 1 Timothy 2:11, 12. What are God's clear commands to women in these two verses?

1. ....

....

2. ....

....

What are to two reasons given why women should not be teachers to men in the churches nor have authority over men?

1. ....

....

2. ....

....

God formed Adam first. Men are the ones that God created to be in authority in the churches and in the homes. I believe they are also to be in authority everywhere else since all of the Priests, Levites, Scribes, Major and Minor Prophets, Kings of Israel and Judah, Patriarchs, Authors of Scripture, Forerunner of Christ (John the Baptist), Christ, Apostles, Elders, and Deacons were men and are to be men. God is clear in His authority structure all throughout the Bible.

The woman, Eve, was deceived. Does this mean that all women are more easily deceived than men? I tend to believe so but I know others disagree. I believe God made the male nature more skeptical and questioning than most women's nature. Why do you think car salesmen prefer to sell cars to women?

God is very clear about women's roles in the church services. Who has God ordained to teach in the churches? Look up 1 Timothy 3:2, 5.

1. ....

....

2. ....

....

God has ordained men to speak and teach in the churches. Women are to be silent. This is repeated FIVE times in the above verses listed. (Yes, we can sing and worship with the congregation! Singing is very different than speaking out and teaching.)

Remind yourself what makes a woman beautiful from 1 Peter 3:4. ....

....

....

....

Learning to be quiet isn't punishment and isn't a bad quality to pursue. It's God's ordained order for the churches. Why according to 1 Corinthians 14:33? ....

....

....

....

....

Write out 1 Thessalonians 5:11.

We are commanded to "study to be quiet." What are some ways that you can do this?

The entire chapter of 1 Corinthians 14 concerns the order of the church services and woman are commanded to be silent. No confusion here! Study this chapter carefully and it will become very clear to you.

Study # 11

MEEK AND QUIET SPIRIT

$\mathcal{M}$ost women do not naturally have a meek and quiet spirit. Our culture promotes women being loud, independent, and doing what they want. This isn't God's will for us, women. Let's study what He has to say about having meek and quiet spirits.

What is the opposite of a meek and quiet spirit given in Proverbs 7:11?

....

....

Write out 1 Peter 3:4.

....

....

....

Meek means "mild of temper; soft; gentle; not easily provoked or irritated; yielding; humble; submissive to the divine will." What do these verses say about the word meek?

Psalm 22:26

....

Psalm 25:9

....

Psalm 37:11

....

Psalm 147:6 ....

....

Psalm 149:4 ....

....

Isaiah 29:19 ....

....

God deeply values meekness. It makes a woman beautiful by being at peace with herself and with others. She's satisfied (content), has good judgment, teachable to God's ways, confident in her eternal future, secure in who she is in Christ, rests in God's finished work in her life, and is full of the joy of the LORD; for the joy of the LORD is her strength!

What words are related to quiet in these verses:

2 Kings 11:20 ....

....

1 Chronicles 4:40 ....

....

Jeremiah 30:10 ....

....

1 Thessalonians 4:11 ....

....

1 Timothy 2:2 ....

....

God also values quietness of spirit. People enjoy being with a woman who has this quality. She doesn't fret nor does she live in fear because she knows God is sovereign over all. She studies to be quiet by consistently meditating upon God's Holy Word and allows Him to transform her life. She leads a quiet and peaceable life in all godliness and contentment.

Study #12
HOMEMAKING

*H*omemaking is a skill that many young women are no longer taught by their mothers since many of them had mothers who were away from home all day at their jobs. Therefore, it's up to the older women to come alongside of the young women and teach them these skills. Homemaking involves working hard in your home and making it a place of comfort, peace, and order for your family.

Along with homemaking, it's good to study nutrition and learn how to keep your family as healthy as you can. There are many other things you can find to do at home, women. It need not ever be boring. Only boring people get bored! Use your creativity to bless your husband and children in your home.

What are your strengths in homemaking?

....

....

....

....

What are your weaknesses in homemaking?

....

....

....

....

In today's culture, homemaking is looked down upon and a lot of it is outsourced for others to do instead because mothers aren't home to do it. Remind yourself that the greatest of all is the servant of all. As you daily serve your husband and children, you are serving Christ. When you serve the guests in your home, likewise, you are serving Christ.

God is a God of order and beauty so our homes should reflect this. He wants us to work hard and whatever we do, we are to do it "heartily as unto the Lord" (Colossians 3:23). We are promised that we will reap what we sow. If we are lazy in our homemaking, our homes will show it but if we are diligent and hard-working in our homes, our homes will show this, too. An uncluttered and clean home is much more pleasant to live in than a dirty, cluttered home. How can you begin to bring order and beauty to your home? It doesn't have to cost much either!

....

....

....

....

....

....

Decide to make your bed every morning and train your children to do likewise. Make sure your home is picked up at night and the kitchen is clean. Start off with small goals and add to them gradually.

Learn to clean as you go. If you see something that needs cleaning, clean it! Some women do better with routines. On Monday, they wash all of the clothes. On Tuesday, they clean the bathrooms. On Wednesday, they dust and oil the furniture. On Thursday, they vacuum and on Friday, they mop. Make one that suits your life.

Train children to clean up after themselves and to help you with household chores. The boys, as they grow older, can help with the outdoor chores. The more you focus upon this when they are young, the easier it will be for you when they are older.

I enjoy an uncluttered home and surfaces that are cleared of things I don't use every day. It makes it a lot easier to clean. I store things under my sinks and in the drawers in my bathrooms. I have very little on the counter. The less stuff we have, the easier it is to keep it clean and organized. Most of us have way more stuff than we need.

Many young women have told me that they simply don't cook and they don't know how. This is a poor excuse to not cook. For one thing, it saves a lot of money to learn to cook food from scratch. For another, it's a whole lot healthier for your family. With all of the YouTubes, cookbooks, and TV cooking shows available, there is no reason that women can't teach themselves to be good cooks. I have all of my tried and true family favorite recipes on my old blog at lorialexander. blogspot.com. They are simple and nutritious. I only cook healthy meals for my family because I know that what we nourish our body with is our fuel. If we put bad gas in our car, it won't run right just as if we put bad food into our body, it won't run right for the long-term.

If you're newly married, consider asking your husband what three things he would like when he gets home, if he works away from home. Then work on accomplishing these things for him! It's another way you can show love to your husband.

It's good to find natural cleaning products to clean with since we want as few toxic chemicals in our home as possible. I use ½ part vinegar, ½ part water, and a squirt of dish soap to clean most things. I use it on mirrors, windows, counter-tops, tables, and all over in the bathrooms. I use plain olive oil on my wood furniture. I have even made my own laundry detergent! It's easy to find ways to clean easily, efficiently, and with no toxic chemicals by scouring the Internet. Be aware of using air fresheners. They are toxic! It's better to keep our homes clean rather than to use air fresheners.

Make a list of five things you want to keep up with every day.

1. ....
   ....

2. ....
   ....

3. ....
   ....

4.
_____

_____

5.
_____

_____

I love what C. S Lewis wrote about homemaking, "The home-maker has the ultimate career. All other careers exist for one purpose only - and that is to support the ultimate career." Never feel inferior as you go about your tasks each day. Know that you are right where God wants you to be!

Conclusion

*I*n these 12 chapters, you have learned all about biblical womanhood and God's will for your lives. Living for Him is a glorious thing, dear women! He is our Creator and He knows what is best for us. This is why we are told that His ways are "good, and acceptable, and perfect" (Romans 12:2).

Does it mean that it's easy to obey what He has commanded of us? No! The path is narrow that we are called to take and few want to travel on it. The Lord tells us, "Stand ye in the ways, and see, and ask for the old paths, where is the good way, and walk therein, and ye shall find rest for your souls" (Jeremiah 6:16). He has not left us alone to walk on this narrow path that leads to life. He has given us His Holy Spirit that we are told works mightily within us (Colossians 1:29). You are not alone in your struggles so remind yourself that you can do ALL things through Christ who strengthens you!

I am 60 years old as I write this book. I have been married for 38 years. I have four grown and married children and am expecting my tenth grandchild this year. I have experienced the Lord's ways and they are very good. I have learned to live in submission to my husband and treat him with kindness. I continue to grow in the wisdom and the knowledge of the LORD by studying His Word almost daily. I have learned to not control others but to love and serve them instead. The fruit is so much sweeter living by God's Word instead of my own selfish ambition and going my own way. I have tasted that the LORD is gracious to me (1 Peter 2:3)!

Looking back on raising my children through years of pain and illness, I can see God's strength and grace covering all those difficult years. He will accomplish what He desires of you and He will give you the grace and the strength to do so. Do not lose hope; for hope is the anchor of the soul (Hebrews 6:19). He promises to never leave nor forsake you so trust Him!

Made in the USA
Coppell, TX
22 June 2021